MARTHA STUART
Excruciatingly Perfect
WEDDINGS

by Tom Connor & Jim Downey

HarperPerennial
A Division of HarperCollinsPublishers

Contents

17

8

36

5

50

26

25

28

Introduction

A wedding is many things.

It is the warm glow that comes from watching lawyers draft a killer pre-nuptial agreement. It is the flash of envy in your unmarried friends' eyes when you announce your engagement. It is the unbridled joy of seeing your net worth quadruple—and being able to stuff your face with reception hors d'oeuvres and desserts—now that he's legally yours.

Planning a wedding begins in childhood. There is much to do and little time for dolls, pets, friends or emotional development, attachments or commitments of any kind.

Grade school affords one of the earliest opportunities to begin prospecting for future husbands. By fifth grade, boys with business acumen will begin to make their presence known. Track them carefully. Beware of booger-flickers and little idiots that can fart the National Anthem. They are the types likely to demand something from you on your honeymoon.

Planning the *perfect* wedding, on the other hand, begins in *my* childhood. As a sixth grader at Our Lady of Suspicious Conception, I organized mock weddings for my classmates, frequently performing the ceremonies myself and arranging marriages of increasingly experimental natures: teachers' pets and detentionees, girls and horses, boys and priests, et cetera. By the time I was ready to wed, I knew exactly what *not* to do.

Perfect or imperfect, all weddings possess moments of great romance and magic.

Many years later, I still remember the magical moments from my wedding: the look of astonishment on the faces of my bridesmaids, all size 12s, as they attempted to squeeze into the size 6 dresses I made for them; the lovely, flaky souvlakia, served at our reception and re-heated a month later for my first catering job; the knowledge that soon I would completely dominate the relationship, checkbook and household.

Of course, each bride will have special memories of her own wedding day. But for a lucky few, one memory above all others will endure the test of time: Long after their husbands have left them for less intelligent, less successful, younger, thinner, sexier wives, they'll remember that I planned their weddings.

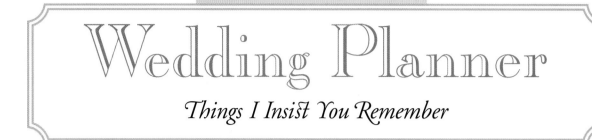

Wedding Planner

Things I Insist You Remember

TWENTY YEARS BEFORE WEDDING

Charge neighborhood children to play "Spin the Bottle"

When "playing" house, pay attention. This is serious business

Read biographies of past marriage masters — Gabor, Taylor, Trump — for tips

Try your wings at ordering boys around

TEN YEARS BEFORE

Evaluate classmates for photogenic wedding mates

Subscribe to my magazine and buy my books

Invest $50,000 in Martha Stuart Living Inc. stock to curry favor

Begin interviewing for wait staff

Contribute funds to Mayor or First Selectperson in your wedding area (local laws will need to be bent)

Begin sincerity lessons

Have parents invest in a champagne grape crop

Choose a law firm

One of the first questions to be asked when planning a wedding is, "Who's wedding is it?" And, if I'm involved, one of the first answers to accept is, "It's mine." This is because you're hopelessly lazy, disorganized and romantic. In fact, you have no business getting engaged in the first place. If you insist, however, here's what you must do:

FIVE YEARS BEFORE WEDDING

Set season and weekend

Reserve every church, temple, hall, friends' estate, private club, ethnic club, restaurant and public site in your area to preempt competition

Buy my wedding-issue magazines, romance organizer, love video, pre-nuptial planner and honeymoon computer program

Indenture Third World seamstresses

Finish hybriding rose named after yourself

THREE YEARS BEFORE

★ Note: I will need to be present for most decisions from this point on

Book me as consultant

Start callbacks for bridesmaids. If your friends don't measure up, we will need to book professional models and actresses

Consult astrologer to determine what kind of music will be popular in three years; audition musicians

Book George Lucas for special effects: early morning fog, starry night, etc.; controlling the weather is a key area!

Arrange to have doppler weather radar installed at wedding site (see above)

ONE YEAR BEFORE WEDDING

Draft pre-nuptials

Book me as caterer

If you have favorite foods or family recipes that you might want to incorporate, forget about them

Select eligible wedding partner

Order series of blood, sperm and
I.Q. tests

Submit fiancé to me for inspection,
testing and approval

Run D&D on future parents-in-law;
check College Board and graduate
school board scores; interview
employer and former lovers, if any

Make honeymoon reservations
for three

Begin wind-sprints for serving staff

Check for stable political atmo-
sphere in honeymoon destination

Choose a Kegel coach

SIX MONTHS
BEFORE WEDDING

Learn fiancé's name

Hire me as officiant

Select readings for ceremony from
the New Testament, *The Prophet, The
Complete Lyrics of Abba,* or *The Best
of Martha Stuart Living*

Order any special lingerie from
Martha's Secret catalog

Try one last time for Beatles
reunion

Send me final $100,000 retainer

Choose attendants; find out sizes;
order dresses three sizes too small
(hee hee)

(see "A Family Wedding")

Stop calling me

THREE MONTHS BEFORE

Ask fiancé for correct spelling of his
name

Assign responsibilities to family
members, friends & hired help;
order staff uniforms for them; hold
random inspections; raise Cain;
mete out appropriate discipline

Order groom's attire; have it look
really stupid

Mail, fax, e-mail engagement
announcement to national and
international papers

Make limousine arrangements for
self; check public transportation
schedule for groom and his relatives

Obtain salmonella cultures to intro-
duce into food of unwanted guests

Pay off local police chief

ONE MONTH BEFORE

Memorize fiancé's name

Draft spontaneous outpourings of
love for groom to recite at altar

Review pre-nuptials with law partners

Draw up seating chart according to
anticipated value of wedding gifts

TWO WEEKS BEFORE

If ceremony or reception is to be held
at parents' home, make sure next-door
neighbors' yards are up to snuff;
remind them of upcoming event by
ramming their gardener against fence
with four-wheel-drive vehicle

ONE WEEK BEFORE

Make gown

Practice saying groom's name

Start Atavan for mother of the bride

Pre-heat all ovens

Start dough on 78th rise

DAY BEFORE

Bake & ice wedding cake (save bowl,
spoons & beater blades for me to lick)

Go out with rugby team one last
night

Polish all ice sculptures

Final rehearsal with actual tears
(glycerine to be used at wedding)

Give all pets and elderly guests
diuretic & laxatives to avoid any
spills during reception

YOUR WEDDING DAY

Pack marital aide and blow-up
groom

THE DAY AFTER
YOUR WEDDING

Invoice guests for reception hors
d'oeuvres, cocktails, dinner and cake
(don't forget to add sales tax)

Mail consummation and marital
performance announcement to
newspapers and wire services

If dissatisfied on wedding night,
begin legal proceedings

Return ring and pocket cash

Transfer title to house and all other
assets to your name

Bouquets

In the beginning, Adam grabbed a handful of wild birds-of-paradise, and grass and leaves and droppings, and tossed them in the general direction of Eve. She picked them up.

In that seminal moment was born a romantic tradition I've kept alive to this day: gathering bouquets of wild — or free-range — flowers wherever I find them. The one improvement I've made upon the ancient floral theme is that I charge nervous young brides and their mothers unnatural amounts of money the morning of the wedding.

For the recent marriage of the daughter of a childhood friend of mine, for instance, I went out into the cutting gardens one day before dawn dressed only in Wellies and gardening gloves, and I picked everything that was in bloom. It was dark, *okay*? How the hell was I supposed to know I'd crossed my property line and cut all of my neighbor's prize-winning roses? So *sue* me. Okay, so sue me again!

No matter where flowers are from, new concepts of couples and marriage have rearranged the very notion of the bridal bouquet. So that when J. Arnold Arnoldson and Joe DiStefano walked down the aisle recently, I filled Joe's arms with a bouquet of erect, long-stamened anthuriums in formal, elbow-length rubber gloves glistening with a fresh application of Valvoline.

For more traditional brides, meanwhile, I frequently suggest bunches of wilted, drooping, decaying roses. What more fitting symbol of where most heterosexual marriages are headed in the '90s?

ABOVE: *What better way to hide horticultural experiments gone awry than to turn them into colorful hats for the bridesmaids. Here, a mutant strain of bird-of-paradise escapes the compost heap to become a bold chapeau that is also useful for opening beer bottles.*

RIGHT: *I find that bridesmaids feel more involved in the wedding process if they're handed pruning shears and several yards of chicken wire, then sent into the garden to make their own dresses.*

I don't know why, but women tend to get headaches in my presence. When that happens during a wedding, it can impart an unwelcome melancholy look to the females in the wedding party. To avoid this occurrence, I have had good luck strapping about four pounds of fresh sunflowers to the bridesmaids' heads with zinc baling wire. The weight of this arrangement shifts the area of pain away from the head and down onto the neck, where eventually it can be massaged away.

The Boutonniere

A corruption of the French term *booty-entrée*, boutonnieres were originally flowers with long stems that were thrust deeply into tight buttonholes of tuxedo jacket lapels. They were first worn in early-16th-century France as a sign to all that the groom was, indeed, the man. By the next century males were jamming large, flowering shrubbery and whole perennial gardens into their lapels to prove the point. Today, as the importance of the groom to the wedding has shriveled, so has the boutonniere — to the extent that the foreshortened stem is now simply run through with a straight pin and affixed to the outside of the lapel. Nevertheless, when handled properly, some boutonnieres still rise to the occasion, if for only a short period of time.

It may be hard to believe, but I have a dark side. Sometimes I put away the cheerful, merry, generous, loving and sweet soul that I am, open the cellar door of my soul and invite my other half up into the world. I believe that, like me, all women have gloriously dismal aspects to their personalities. Above is, shall we say, an alternative look for the bride on one of those "special days."

Pre-Nups

*I*n this day and age, writing a solid, airtight pre-nuptial is in many ways more important than saving your virginity. This totally bullet-proof document will insure happiness and security for the bride when the inevitable happens and her marriage fails. The following is an example of what I would consider a good basic pre-nuptial agreement:

★ THIS DOCUMENT IS ★ 100% BULLET-PROOF

SEAL OF CERTIFICATION

MARTHA STUART

(YOUR NAME HERE) VS (TO WHOM IT MAY CONCERN):

To the attorneys of the groom, the groom, the groom's family and the groom's family's family:

In the event that the Bride shall perceive any feelings of doubt, unhappiness, disquietude or displeasure within the sacred confines of this marriage, she has the unlimited option to a hasty uncontested divorce.

Within one hour of her decision to divorce, a cashier's check will be written to the Bride for the sum total of the groom's liquid assets including all pension funds and cash in his accounts.

The family homes will be deeded over to the Bride immediately, all contents included with the exception of the domestic animals which will be picked up with posthaste and delivered to the groom's mother.

Groom shall refrain from invoking the Bride's name in any conversation or in the media. The Bride shall have unlimited rights to editorialize her version of the events of the marriage for sale to any entity willing to pay.

For five years, the Bride will have unlimited charging privileges at any store that advertises in V*ogue, Harper's Bazaar*, or *Is Martha Stuart Living?*

All the mutual friends of the Bride and groom shall continue to send birthday gifts and Christmas presents to the Bride in perpetuity.

All automobiles shall be delivered to the Bride immediately and shall be detailed daily and replaced yearly.

La Côte Basque will deliver three meals a day to the Bride during her period of mourning (three years)

A round-the-clock psychotherapist will be retained for the well-being of the Bride and any of her friends.

Neiman Marcus will put on a fashion and fur showing in the Bride's home at intervals of no longer than every four weeks.

Richard Simmons will be retained for positive reinforcement.

Any complaining by the ex-husband, his family or his family's family shall be considered a breach of this agreement.

If the Bride decides to marry again, this agreement shall remain in effect until the Bride decides that she shall keep her next husband or for two years, whichever comes first. At that time the agreement will be transferred to the new groom and his family.

May this marriage be blessed.

Arranging Music

Music is one of the most romantic and memorable elements of a wedding. I have no idea why. It's also the most musical, I'm told.

Each bride brings to her wedding her own musical tastes and experiences. Growing up, I enjoyed listening to field hollers and Polish kielbasa stuffing jingles. Later, in college in the 60s, I was swept up in the bands that were expanding our consciousness and changing the world. So that when it came time to arrange the music for my own wedding, I made a selection based on my personal taste and generation. I booked Bread.

Today, brides like Winifred Drexel Diddle prefer traditional society bands such as The Peter Dooshman Big Band or The Whiffenpoufs. Others, like Susan Ripschitz, insist on newer, more alternative groups: Youth in Asia, for example, or Sucking Chest Wound.

Often, it is economically wise to hire a young band found on the streets, in the subways or on the bathroom floor of a club like Monkey Head Ribbon. It is always wise to hire fresh, new groups such as, oh, I don't know, Martha and the Vendettas, for example—an all-girl, middle-aged, bitter, divorcée, suburban, soul/rap/lecture group out of Connecticut.

When making arrangements for a band or orchestra, allow several years' time and include contractual clauses covering every contingency from loss of lyric memory due to the onset of Alzheimer's to death caused by coronary, overdose or playing "We've Only Just Begun" one too many times.

Now in its sixth decade of performing, Hell Toupee is one of the most popular society wedding orchestras in New Jersey. Be sure to book them at least an hour in advance, then hire a backup orchestra: Drummer Skippy Budner has developed a serious prune dependency in recent years which has made it difficult for him to be very far away from a restroom, thus causing occasional musicus interruptus. Yet no band on the circuit knows more versions of "Feelings."

OPPOSITE, TOP: *A bold and occasionally unbathed new wave of musical groups may be found "playing" society weddings today. No matter what the "tempo," though, old monied guests retain the tradition of remaining motionless while dancing for fear of exposing their hereditary lack of rhythm.*

OPPOSITE, BOTTOM: *Despite the prevalence of popular alternative wedding bands such as Blunt Instrument, Sucking Chest Wound and Youth in Asia (pictured), older guests still tend to be surprised when encountering musicians other than Lester Lanolin and members of his orchestra.*

ABOVE: *A popular all-female rap/lecture group, Martha and the Vendettas has earned respect on the suburban wedding circuit for its information-packed lyrics, precision dancing and raw aggression in collecting performance fees.*

Top Society Bands

Martha and the Vendettas

The Peter Dooshman Orchestra

The Lester Lanolin Orchestra

Hell Toupee Orchestra

The Glen Miller Band

The Mitch Miller Band

The Steve Miller Band

The Whiffenpouffs

Youth in Asia

Martha's Wedding Favorites

Deutschland Uber Alles

My Way

I Enjoy Being a Girl

I'm Gonna Wash That Man
Right Out of My Hair

It's My Party
(and you'll cry if I want you to)

Fifty Ways to Lose Your Husband

Stop! In the Name of Love

I Am Woman

The Way You Cook Tonight

If the bride's parents have money, and by that I mean real money — disposable, spendable, gorgeous, blue money — then there is no choice but to book a society dance band for the reception. Finding a great band is hard because all the wonderful band leaders of yesteryear have long since played their last coda. There is one legend still available when he is conscious: the marvelous Peter Dooshman.

As the evening wears on, Peter typically plays his signature arrangement of "The Days of Wine and Rosé" until the last dancers have left and he is simply collapsing with happiness.

Invitations

I understand advertising. I invented "spin." No one knows the power of a well-turned phrase better than I. Besides, everybody who's worth a shit shows up at every wedding I throw. Having said that, if you want all the right people to attend your wedding, you'd better make your invitations sing like the sirens on the proverbial shore. The following are a few starter ideas that have worked well for me in the past:

America's Hostess — Martha Stuart — insists

on your presence at the marriage and incorporation of

(Your Name Here) to (His Name Here).

Guests will arrive no later than 11:00 a.m. on Saturday, June 6, 1998,

under penalty of exclusion and banishment from all future family events.

❧

Guests shall bring new, wrapped wedding gifts

appraised by Sotheby's or Christie's at a value of

no less than $1,000.00 American.

Guests agree to eat no more than one portion of food and

to imbibe no more than 6 oz. of alcoholic beverages.

❧

All guests will clean their immediate area and leave

the premises in an orderly fashion no later than 3 p.m.

Join us in this joyous celebration of love!

R.S.V.P.

MarthaStuartDomesticProductionsWorldwideIndustries@Dominatrix.com

His Holiness Pope John,
in association with Mr. & Mrs. Winton Twiggy-Botham,
requests the pleasure of your company
at the wedding of their daughter
Penelope.

To be held at Vatican West
(formerly Spazio's Catering Hall & Roller Rink)

Sunday, June 14, in the year of the Lord 1998, 3:00 p.m.

The Pope (or a substitute)
will be taking individual confessions
before hors d'oeuvres at the reception.

R.S.V.P.

Mailboxes Are Us, Rte. 9 , Paramus, New Jersey

Nick Jagger and the Rolling Stoans are playing at a wedding for
Miss Judy ("I Can't Get No Satisfaction") Blumenthal
and Sid "Vicious" Clapman.

To be held at Yankee Stadium
(or the Blumenthal home if the game goes into extra innings)

June 27, 1998, 6:00 p.m.

The Stoans will alternate sets with Krosby Stilles & Nashman.
So bring your dancin' shoes.
Also bring any food or beverage that you will require.

R.S.V.P. SidVicious@aol.com.

Preparations

I prepare for a wedding much the same way I do for a business meeting, White House invitation, court date or data date: with complete and utter command of every aspect of the event, and a Stalin-like execution of the details.

Important decisions early in the planning stage include what currency I'll be paid in, which leftovers from my show and magazine shoots will be served at the reception, who will be my date at the wedding and where will we be going on your honeymoon.

Not to be overlooked in all the consulting and catering is the bridal gown, which, if you want it to be perfect — and you do want it to be perfect — you must make yourself (see page 30). I can rent you the sheep (by the day) and the spinning wheel (by the hour), but after that you're on your own.

The most important preparation for any wedding guest is deciding what to throw at the bride and groom after the ceremony. In the past, I have had great success with a mixture of wild groats and an Iraqi bulgur wheat that explodes upon contact. Lately, however, I'm finding that the basic black-eyed pea, along with a brand of rock candy I buy in Detroit, deliver the same message but with less traceability (see "Throwables," page 28).

Now, after planning scads of individual weddings, the only challenge left for me is to plan everyone's wedding, all at once. Currently, then, I'm organizing a mass wedding of some 10,000 brides who've hired me to help plan their weddings. Each one believes that I am her sole personal consultant, that she is the center of my professional attention and that she will be married in the presence of only her family and friends. The little fools.

Homemade Wedding Cake

Nothing is quite so fulfilling for a bride as making the wedding cake herself.

To ensure its freshness, begin baking 24 hours before the reception. And to memorialize

your cake in a highly personal way, here's an original decorative icing idea of mine.

Table Settings

FIDDLEHEAD FERN FORK

PORK TARTARE FORK

SQUID DE-VEINER

WHIFFENPOUFF POST-PRANDIAL TUNING FORK

FERRET KNIFE

WILD BOAR TAUNTING & TENDERIZING FORK

BITCH FORK

FAT SKIMMING KNIFE

TUNING FORK

RUMP ROAST POKING FORK

EAR WAX FORK

RETINA FORK

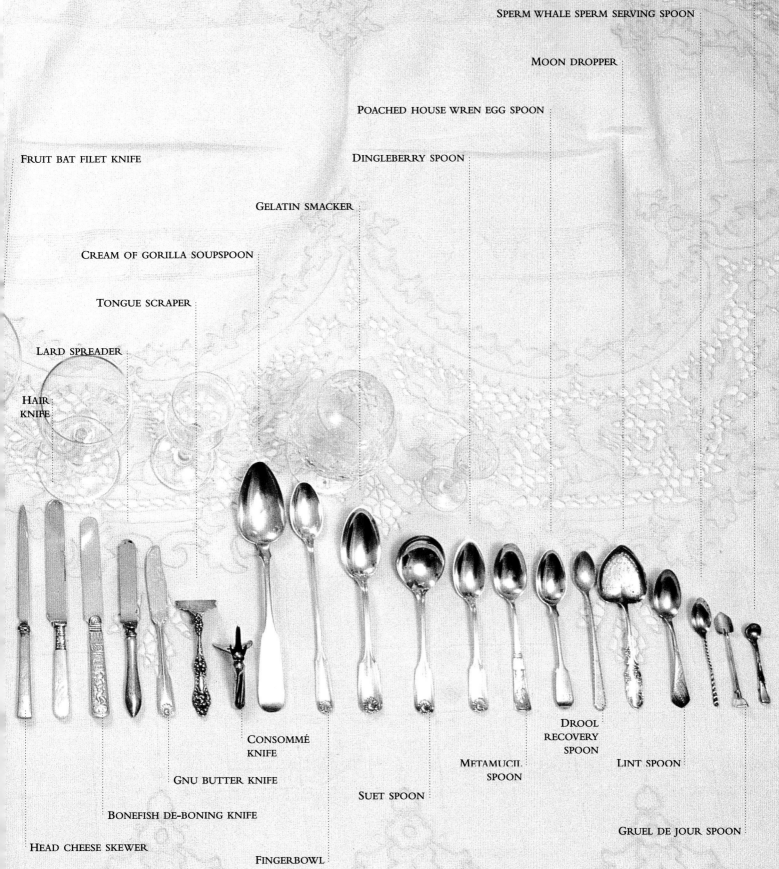

PEARL SCOOP

SPERM WHALE SPERM SERVING SPOON

MOON DROPPER

POACHED HOUSE WREN EGG SPOON

FRUIT BAT FILET KNIFE

DINGLEBERRY SPOON

GELATIN SMACKER

CREAM OF GORILLA SOUPSPOON

TONGUE SCRAPER

LARD SPREADER

HAIR KNIFE

CONSOMMÉ KNIFE

DROOL RECOVERY SPOON

GNU BUTTER KNIFE

METAMUCIL SPOON

LINT SPOON

SUET SPOON

BONEFISH DE-BONING KNIFE

GRUEL DE JOUR SPOON

HEAD CHEESE SKEWER

FINGERBOWL SOUPSPOON (HEE HEE)

Throwables

red kidney bean
shrapnel

50-millimeter
fava beans

rock salt

high-speed,
anti-personnel
groats

black-eyed
peas

wilding rice

The Aerodynamics of Love

I don't know when the first handful of rice was thrown at a newly married couple, but I personally felt the painful sting of the basmati at my own wedding. At that moment, I realized that throwing things at a young, blushing bride, all aglow with her life ahead of her, can be great fun—and, if well thrown, can make a powerful statement as well.

The key here is control. One doesn't want to make wild pitches that miss the bride completely and scar the corneas of everyone on the other side of the aisle, thereby opening up endless possibilities for lawsuits. Perfect control can be achieved only after hundreds of hours on your throwing range using, say, a gardener as a target.

Today, there are a multitude of alternate throwables. Rock candy is particularly painful. Fava beans have a very unpredictable flight path. And kidney beans can be easily confused with a swarm of stinging bees. Develop a slider, a sinker and a reliable change-up, and you will leave your mark as well as an unforgettable memory for the bride.

I use a Hoffstedtler tungsten steel file on each grain to duplicate the stinger of the African killer bee.

Since my skin is thick, I test each wicked little point for proper "bite."

Check the aerodynamics carefully. It helps to visualize each grain as a miniature harpoon—and the bride as the White Whale.

When properly hurled, wild rice makes lovely patterns on a glowing cheek.

A Handmade Gown

The nineties have given us a brave new world of materials from which to choose fabulous bridal gowns. Thermal fleece, ballistic Kevlar, aluminized rayon, Space Age seran wrap, graphite, gunite, rubber, leather, latex, dolphin skin, baby Naugahyde sheep's intestinal lining. All of these are acceptable, even fashionable, today.

I still have the gown in which my Grandmother Kompulski was wed. It is a classic, Old World gown of homemade muslin and hardened tapioca she'd stitched together herself, with a bustle fashioned from a prize-winning cabbage and a 300-yard burlap train, all laid over a muskrat petticoat and crinolines of real skin. I wear it from time to time on dates.

Despite all the changes taking place in society in the last decade, the classics have endured. And nothing is more classic than a traditional handmade gown, preferably of cotton and, unavoidably, one you've made yourself.

Since commercial cotton is usually weevilly and picked by unattractive machines or people, you must grow your own. To yield enough high-quality cotton for wedding day stockings, panties, petticoat, crinolines, chastity belt, sanitary napkins, makeup cotton balls and sleeve tissues, the first thing you'll need is a minimum of five acres of open land. The soil must be a sandy loam with ten to twelve percent ochre clay content mulched over with an even three inches of aged mule manure.

Simply pick, clean, cardle, spindle, warp, windle and thread the raw cotton through your spinning wheel, as close to the hour of the wedding as possible. And when you walk up that aisle, you'll understand the kind of deep satisfaction I feel — all of the time.

A Handmade Gown

Here I pick over the late summer crop in time to make fall panties for myself and my closest friends. This is my cotton.

Many people believe they're doing a bride a favor when they perform every task and errand for them. This is so wrong. The best thing one can do for a young woman on the verge of the most important day of her life is to take her mind off the event by putting a Martha-like load in her washing machine. At right, following my strong suggestion, a bride-to-be attempts to finish a simple little cotton gown just hours before the ceremony. However, if you look closely, as I have, you'll notice that she's missed a stitch on row 28 and will have to start over from scratch.

Bridesmaids

They've been your closest friends since childhood and college.

When you got your period during gym in junior high, they were there to throw things to you (or at you) in the showers. When your boyfriend in high school dumped you for Candy Meeks, who had breasts the size of Crenshaw melons, they were there to console you with the fact that your head was bigger than hers. When you got caught cheating on your Home Ec final in college, they were the ones who advised you to drop out and get married rather than graduate. Come to think of it, they've pissed you off at almost every stage of your life, and you've never forgotten it.

But now you need them. Because if grooms are occasionally necessary, bridesmaids are indispensable. They laugh and cry with you, envy you, go shopping and drinking with you, throw up for you. Or should.

And when it comes time to repay your bridesmaids for everything they've ever done, there's no better way than to make the very dresses they will wear. One of my fondest memories of my own wedding was designing and sewing my bridesmaids' dresses — each four sizes too small! I can still hear their pork-like squealings as they attempted to squeeze those bodies to go into those dresses the way forcemeat gets stuffed into sausage casing.

If you can, take a few minutes on your wedding day to hide in the room where your bridesmaids will be changing into the dresses you made for them (see "Wedding Planner," page 6). Nothing quite relieves pre-nuptial tensions like a deep, heartfelt laugh.

I like to relieve the stress of wedding preparations by making all of the bridesmaids' dresses two to four sizes too small. Laughter at someone else's expense is the best medicine.

A Family Wedding

The tears of a blushing bride, the terror of the groom as he contemplates his future, the envy of the guests as they covet a lifestyle they can never attain. These are but a few of the delicious pleasures of a family wedding.

When a relative of mine asked me to assume command of her "special day," I was, of course, thrilled. Not only would this be a superb networking opportunity, but I could count it as a tax write-off, a wedding present and a profit center.

For me, at this point in my life, the idea of getting married is somewhere below paying the groundskeeper on my list. A tiny part of me, though, enjoys helping a couple who spent ten minutes together on spring break make a life-long commitment.

Running a wedding is a festival of delights. It's a chance to control guests and discipline children, a chance to berate workers and an opportunity to dominate the Bride and Groom. These golden moments, when everybody around me is performing like perfectly trained circus dogs, are the real reasons that life, as I live it, is good.

Even when a strict dress code has been mandated, some guests simply refuse to comply. When the groom's aunt and uncle drove, uninvited, all the way from Sparkling Window, Texas, to attend, I sequestered them in a different part of the property and used the car for a nice touch of red in the bushes.

I take every opportunity to eliminate choices for the guests. Normally a group this large would have at least twenty people in unattractive, less-than-tasteful clothing. The problem was easily solved by making everyone dress exactly like me.

Don't let your guests wander the reception, randomly having fun and leading to moblike behavior. Instead, lock them into meticulously choreographed routines that are time-consuming and make for better pictures. Here, I work the women until they perfect an acceptable minuet.

What to Do with Unwanted Guests

As far as I'm concerned, unless I personally make up the guest list, most guests are unwanted. But since they are there anyway, they must be dealt with. If your property is big enough, you can simply throw another party out of sight of the main party and have the traffic monitor steer all the undesirables there.

Another option is to catch the unwanteds at the off-ramp and send them to another wedding or state, thereby setting up the ideal scenario wherein the gifts will arrive by mail and the guests will already have gone home in frustration.

Here the parents of the groom, ejected from the wedding party for defying my dress code, dance to the distant strains of "You Light Up My Life" on a lawn several houses away.

A Family Wedding

Always the caterer, never the catered to.

Kids will be kids, which is why I do my best

to exclude them from the weddings I plan.

When they manage to whine their way in,

trouble is certain to follow.

After a prank in which my hors d'oeuvres suffered a nasty spill, an employee of Stuart Domestic Security detains youthful suspects prior to questioning and booking.

When you mix two disparate families at one occasion, you are simply asking for trouble. Ethnicity, economic strata, black sheep, etc., can all rear their head and ruin a perfectly planned reception. To keep warfare to a minimum, I have found that a selection of anti-depressants and anti-anxiety medications, when taken with liberal amounts of cheap champagne, will calm things down considerably. I realize that this practice will be frowned upon by practically everyone. But since I've got the car keys and it's my party, tough!

What could be more romantic than the rosy glow of homemade beeswax candles at dusk? In this light, the women look lovely and the men less visible. I suggest using them by the hundreds on every table. Sometimes, naturally, a lummox will catch on fire. Yet if he is wearing a white cotton shirt, as per instructions, the flames will look lovely and the blast from the fire extinguisher will add excitement and a lingering, romantic haze.

My Coeur de Bovine, or cattle heart, appetizer serves up to 100 guests and, when properly presented, slams home a cautionary tale to any guest contemplating marriage.

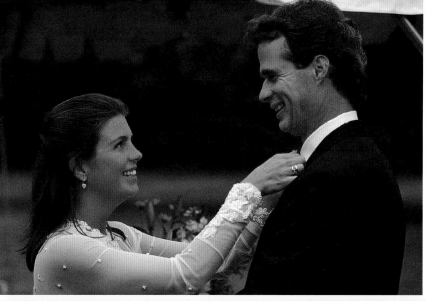

It is natural for a bride to think she knows her man and can administer to his every need. But Martha knows best. Here, I'm simply showing the bride the proper way to tie a bowtie. When she failed to follow my example and I was forced to correct her, she threw an absolute hissy fit.

There is no creature on earth more territorial than a newly minted bride. She still thinks of the groom as her knight in shining armor. She still sees the future as a blissful sequence of charming events from painless consummation, to painless childbirth, to acceptance in the country club and then peaceful death during sleep. Ha!

Here I amuse the crowd with a small
divertissement I was asked to create
for Jake the Snake of the
World Wrestling Federation.

I always keep my temper under the strictest control, using practices taught to me by the late Mother Teresa and the exiled Dalai Lama. But when pushed too far, the decision to defend myself is out of my hands and I switch to the skills taught to me by Mike Tyson and Chuck Norris.

Menus & Recipes

Wedding food — whether for a wedding day breakfast, bridesmaids' brunch, family lunch, family dunch (late afternoon lunch) or rehearsal dinner — is ordained by one thing and one thing only: that it be prepared from recipes found in my books, magazine, syndicated shows, TV specials, CD-ROMs, Web page or 900 number.

For as someone once said, I am the "arbiter of taste" (perhaps my publicist said it, I don't remember, who the hell cares?). What this most likely means is that I get to decide what tastes good — or what looks as though it could taste good — and therefore should be served at a wedding.

Take, for example, the Roulade D'Argent on page 57 of this book. Does it taste good? Technically, no. If you must know, it tastes like newspaper that's been marinated in dumpster juices for a fortnight, then baked for ten hours on the manifold of a '89 Chrysler LeBaron. But that's hardly the point. How does it look? Sinfully rich and deliciously decadent.

One final note on wedding food. When you do use one of my recipes, be sure to factor in a royalty payment to me of fifteen percent per serving (as established and strictly monitored and enforced by MSCAP).

A sculpted ice heart crushing delicate spring flowers
sets the tone for a wedding feast I recently catered.

FOWL BUFFET

SERVES 24

A traditional English bachelor party feast dating back to the Colonial era and still prepared in American suburbs that have remained loyal to the Crown. Where the ingredients have not been available on the national market, I have gone overseas or bred them myself.

1 American eagle

1 dodo bird

1 crested loon

1 mourning dove

1 mockingbird

1. Feed livestock Brie and risotto for a week before the rehearsal dinner party.

2. Line up the fowl, preferably outdoors, in the order you want them to appear on the table.

3. Walk slowly behind the birds, moving from largest to smallest and wacking each in turn in the back of the head with a latrine shovel or other handy garden tool, being careful not to damage the tool (for the larger fowl I recommend a Sheffield sod spade).

4. Use a Bindorrf Turbo 7000 weed-whacker on the high setting to remove feathers and trim excess fat. (Note: An alternative method is to use the weed-whacker first, then spread seed from the barn to the kitchen and, maintaining the same order, walk the birds into the oven.)

5. Roast in same pan in an industrial oven at 175°F for a fortnight, basting at two-hour intervals with their own juices or any other creatures' juices at your disposal.

Poultry Sum

All spring I listened to the bird outside my kitchen window whistle a bad rendition of "Mockingbird Hill." Day after day after day it sang, over and over and over and over, distracting me from my work and thwarting my attempts to roust it from its roost.

Finally in June, I was presented with the right occasion for making culinary use of this insulting pile of feathers. I also discovered an effective method for bringing it from tree to table (napalm imparts to poultry an interesting undertaste, too). As with the past mockingbird shown in the photograph on the facing page, all of the fowl on the menu for the Ripschitz wedding reception have offended me in one way or another over the years.

In planning dinner for a special occasion, keep a hit list of poultry that have wronged you. I think you'll be pleasantly surprised at how quickly they can add up to a menu.

BABY CARP SUSHI IN RICE ROLLS
SERVES 10

Carp are low-life, bottom-feeding omnivores found in stagnant ponds and some office water coolers. As hors d'oeuvres, the spawn are showing up with increasing frequency at wedding receptions in Washington and Hollywood.

4 dozen (or 8 pet store takeout cartonful) live infant carp

1 pound off-white or slightly used rice

¼ cup non-virgin oil

1 large bunch local pond vegetation or assorted green plastic aquarium "greens"

1. Keep fish in aquarium until a few minutes before serving.

2. Pour rice in boiling pond water and cook until the consistency of Mob-controlled-grade concrete.

3. Mold hot rice into cylinders in kitchen help's hand, then wrap in damp sea lettuce (if unavailable, I use sections of black leaf disposal bags).

4. Combine oil, spices and the sweat of 10 fishermen and pour over rice.

5. Remove carp individually from water by casting dry flies on the surface (Abercrombie & Fitch carry miniature rods, reels and creels) or together by seine-hauling the aquarium.

6. Wrestle finned beasts onto wet kitchen counter and touch with bare ends of wire plugged into your emergency generator until semi-conscious and no longer thrashing.

7. Lasso tail fins with #3 monofilament line and pull through top of rice rolls so that they resemble '64 Caddies sticking nose-out of the sand; anchor fish to bottom of rolls with .08-gauge sinkers.

8. Stick aquarium "greens" into rice.

9. Serve still slightly twitching.

CLAMS MARTHA

SERVES 40

Basically, this recipe calls for you to find clams with the longest thingies, then chop them off and eat them, it's as simple as that.

Shaker-style clamming rake and hand-woven reed clamming basket

1 pair green or yellow rubber Smellingtons clamming boots

1 pair khaki clamdiggers

1 white boat-neck undershirt

1 blue denim clamming shirt worn open with sleeves rolled up

4 bushels bigneck clams, harvested that morning

Assorted knives, scissors, surgical instruments and cigar clippers

1 gallon Martha's cocktail sauce

1. Go down to the beach at low tide and first light to catch the little pissers coming out of the mud.

2. Grab them by their thingies.

3. With very sharp instrument, snip off their thingies.

4. Throw away the clams.

5. Eat the thingies.

Martha's Edited Alphabet Soup

ROULADE D'ARGENT (Money Roll)

SERVES 24

I can't stress enough how important it is that the food you serve leaves the guests feeling as if you live a much better life than they do. To accomplish that task, what could be better tthan to serve actual currency. This envy-provoking dish was taught to me by the Baroness Ziggy Thurn und Taxes of Switzerland who literally burns money.

10 pounds freshly snared Thomson's Gazelle meat

2 cups sour goat cheese

11 heads organic garlic

Stack of fresh dollar bills

1. Snare a gazelle on your property. Use skin to make Day-Runner covers, entrails for pudding and send horn stumps off to China to sell for use as aphrodisiac. Slice off a rump roast.

2. Brown the roast over an indoor wood fire in a titanium skillet.

3. Alternate layers of goat cheese and dollar bills.

4. Roll into a roll using a roller.

5. Make four hundred and twenty evenly spaced $1/8$" incisions in the roast using a tungsten carbide surgical scalpel.

6. Insert garlic cloves in incisions.

7. Bake in in-ground pit for 48 hours.

8. Garnish with crisp currency.

9. Sprinkle with pocket change (optional).

MARTHA'S EDITED ALPHABET SOUP

SERVES 24

At lunchtime in the Catholic school I attended as a girl, the nuns running the school, the Sisters of Mussolini, would make us spell out the names of the saints in our alphabet soup before we could have a single spoonful. Later, I refined this valuable educational lesson by making my lunchmates spell my name before they ate. Nowadays, of course, I don't have time to spell my whole name. Besides, it's no longer necessary: I've copyrighted the letter "M" to represent me and me alone.

Six 10" by 22" sheets of raw pasta

30 pounds Big Boy tomatoes from the garden

Entire contents of lemon basil garden

Entire contents of garlic patch

1 pinch from every container in spice rack

8 gallons holy water

1. Roll pasta sheets to uniform $\frac{1}{16}$-inch thickness.

2. With children's scissors or X-Acto knife, cut a dozen alphabets out from sheets; hang letters on clothesline to harden and dry.

3. Now remove all letters except "M"s and feed useless letters to literate staff.

4. Peel, cut and puree tomatoes in blender, picking out the seeds.

5. Throw puree and seasonings into large pot of roiling holy water.

6. Simmer for 3 days and 4 nights.

7. Add letters for last 10 minutes or until an "M" can be thrown against a guest's forehead and stick.

*Note: If your local market does not carry cans of Martha's Edited Alphabet Soup, please let me know. I'll have the manager fired on the spot!

"IN THE MOOD" WEDDING NIGHT HORS D'OEUVRES

SERVES 3

You've planned the romantic evening perfectly. He's liberally "sauced" and he appears to be ready for "harvesting." But sometimes men, idiots that they are, miss every amorous clue you put in front of their bulbous noses. If this hors d'oeuvres recipe doesn't do the trick, there's a strong possibility that he might not be interested in someone of your gender.

Baby corn

Pitted olives

Stiff baby asparagus

Cherry tomatoes

1. Take a baby corn and massage it with any kind of oil until you feel it is ready.

2. Ever so gently, insert it into the hole of a soft, succulent, fully opened black olive.

3. Push it back and forth if necessary until it penetrates completely.

4. Take a nice stiff baby asparagus and stroke off any veins or bumps with your nails.

5. Make a vertical slit in a slightly overripe cherry tomato. Rub the shaft of the asparagus in the slit to get it moist, then shove it into the opening.

6. Serve in bed after a magnum of champagne.

MINI-GOURMETTE FILETTE DE BOEUF MINUSCULE

SERVES 100

This meal is absolutely perfect for the bride on a strict budget. If anyone asks what was served at the reception, the answer is filet mignon. Just not a lot (cost per person = thirty-nine cents).

    100 1.006-ounce filet mignons

    100 small new potatoes

    300 stalks baby asparagus

1. Sear 100 filettes in a 12" antique iron skillet.

2. Boil all 100 potatoes in a saucepan.

3. Blanch the asparagus.

4. Arrange very carefully on small plates (for scale).

LA PETITE PUFFETTE

SERVES 100

The perfect dessert to accompany filette de boeuf (cost per person = two cents).

    1 quart Belgian extra-extra-extra heavy whipping cream

    1 pound pure cane sugar

    100 Dunkin' doughnut holes

1. Whip cream by hand for four hours or until it forms rigid peaks.

2. Fold in sugar with a zebrawood spatula until totally dissolved (about a day).

3. Stuff cream mixture into a large (pony size) veterinary inseminator.

4. Squirt into doughnut holes and serve.

*One per person. Mint optional — can be stolen from neighbor's garden at no charge.

Retractions

How best to phrase this?

Sometimes we say things we don't really mean, like "I do." Sometimes we do things we probably shouldn't do. Like "I do." Sometimes we get married.

Does this mean we shouldn't enjoy planning a wedding or eating and drinking our brains out at the reception? Of course it doesn't. Does it mean we shouldn't spend tens of thousands shopping for an occasion that's clearly doomed from the start? Don't be stupid. Must we return the gown, ring, trousseau, wedding gifts, trust fund, apartment, Chevy Suburban and country house? Try prying them from our cold, dead fingers.

Retraction, separation, divorce, nullification, liquidation — you get the idea: Move on, and quickly, without giving up the spoils of love.

Legally, saying "see ya" to a marriage can be relatively simple and painless.

My advice is always to have an attorney give the bride away, and another lawyer from the firm to read the pre-nuptial agreement in between the call-and-response section of the marriage ceremony. I also like to come along on honeymoons and to drop in unannounced during the first few years of a marriage, in preparation for being called as a witness.

As to dividing fairly those objects of domestication that may possess emotional value but no net worth, such as photographs and pets, I recommend using a TurboGal 911 chain-saw.

It is in the area of the social graces, however, that a split can be sticky. The most graceful way I know of broaching the subject of "I loathe you" is to say to a spouse, directly and caringly, "Look, what we had was very special, but now the reception is over and I have to get on with my life. Is there anything of yours you wanted before I have the locks changed, Tod, I mean Ted?"

If you aren't as comfortable with confrontation as I am, here's a more decorous way of saying essentially the same thing. Serve him Martha's Bitter-Chocolate Au Revoir cake with boysenberry-plasma filling, shown right.

Forget about the recipe. Presentation is everything.

Thanks

Our thanks as always to Linda Downey & Jacey Haskell; Lisa & Jack Connor; Richard & Betty Dorso; Gertrude & the late Tom Connor; Bill & Mary Jo Cornell; George & Del Grenadier; and Carol O'Rourke.

Our extreme gratitude to peerless photographer J. Barry O'Rourke, and to the wonderful Suzi Pemperton and Laura Campbell.

Thanks also to all those who contributed to this book: *Cake-toppers:* Dale Elsessei. *Bouquets & gardens:* Peter Stephens & Chris Lennon of Elegant Effects in Fairfield, Conn., and to Alex Briggs & Docia Naff. *Music:* Frank Nosal & the late Leo Ott (Hell Toupee), Vera Nosal & everyone at the Greenfield Hill Grange, and Monique Hart, formerly of Comedy Central; Chris Smith (The Peter Dooshman Orchestra) and Jackie, Hilary Reid, Peter Callahan; Scott, Aleigha, Audra & Parker Whitmore; Tom, Jim, Bill & Phil (Youth in Asia); and dancers Fran & Dennis Bresnan, Tim & Joanna Smith, David Horvath, Brook Fulton, Jim & Louise Baldwin, young Sophie & Peter Briggs, and grand dame Shirley Smith; and to Vicki Linnartz, Sabrina & Mary Ann Heine (Martha & the Vendettas). *Preparations:* Katricia Navarra ("Throwables"); Jennifer Falcone Mitchell ("A Handmade Gown"); Susie Parks, Lulu Dunn, Debby Ward, Julie & friend ("Bridesmaids").

Family Wedding: Bride Pam Jardim, groom Peter Corrigan, and guests Peter Kappel, Jack Connor, Christian Carrera, Leah Barlow; Kate, George, Casey, Bill & Kim Coleman; Ted, Mary, Teddy, Katie & Elizabeth Youngling; Liz, Andrew & Nicky Youngling; Tom Barry; Karen Connelly; Patty, Ron & Gabriella Rudolph; Dean Builter; Stacey & Jack Cohane; Steve & Sue Sullivan; Jill Ivers, Nina Bates; Larry & Donna Vitalano; Francesco Da Rosa, Katie Hughes, Patty Klein, Linda Smart; Gretchen & Larry Whipple; Audrey & Ira Tumpowski; Sarah & Alene LaMendola; Mary Kate Cohane, Brendan Cohane; Lorri & Joe DeFelice; Diane & Brendan Fisk; Cindy & Mike Herrington; Kathy & Gary Rafsky; Bernelle Stephens; Carole & Marty Wonsiewicz; Gerard & Debra Huerta. *Catering:* Joanne Bilyard.

Hors d'ouevres, entrées, icing & food styling: John Carafoli, Dabney Odge, Alex Briggs and John Savarino. *Props, styling & locations:* Special thanks to Alex Briggs and to Barry & Carol O'Rourke; Barbara Latham; Alison Craig; Maypop Lane in Sandwich, Mass., Just Like Home in Sagamore, Mass.; and to Gerard Huerta for the cherry '55 T-Bird.

In Southport, thanks to Libby Hibbs; Carol Pietrzak-Kish and our friends at The Pequot Library; Mike "Mow" Crescehta and Chief Al; Penthouse Wig Salon; and, as always, to Glenn Oesterle at Village Hardware and Jack & Jerry Ringle at Switzer's Pharmacy. In Westport, thanks to Stanley Klein & all our friends at Klein's of Westport.

Special thanks to agent extraordinaire Joel Fishman, and to Marcella Ziesmann and Kevin Lange of The Bedford Book Works, Inc.; and to Mauro DiPreta, Susan Weinberg and Molly Hennessey at HarperPerennial.

A final thanks—and we do mean final—to the real Martha. Never change, baby.